FILLED WITH THE SPIRIT

Understanding God's
Power in Your Life

BY

JOYCE MEYER

Harrison House
Tulsa, Oklahoma

05 04 03 02 01   08 07 06 05 04 03 02 01

Filled with the Spirit:
Understanding God's Power in Your Life
ISBN 1-57794-406-2
Copyright © 2001 by Joyce Meyer
Life In The Word, Inc.
P. O. Box 655
Fenton, Missouri 63026

Published by Harrison House, Inc.
P.O. Box 35035
Tulsa, Oklahoma 74153

Contents

Introduction

INTRODUCTION

In my years of ministry, I have learned that there are many people who do not fully understand the baptism of the Holy Spirit and how to use and enjoy the gifts of the Spirit. Some people are not even sure the baptism of the Holy Spirit is for them.

I believe in the baptism of the Holy Spirit, and in this book I hope to be able to explain to you why, as I share with you my own experience and the experience and teaching of others through the Scriptures.

Before the Lord gave me the revelation of the present-day ministry of the Holy

Spirit, I didn't really comprehend that the Holy Spirit is a Person. I always referred to the Spirit as "It." I would ask people, "Did you receive 'It'?" But I am happy to tell you that the Holy Spirit is much more than that.

The Holy Spirit is the third Person of the Trinity; He is the power of God. His multiple role as Comforter, Counselor, Helper, Intercessor, Advocate, Strengthener and Standby[1] can be summarized by saying that His purpose is to come into us with His abiding Presence and power and help us do things with ease that would otherwise be hard or even impossible.

We receive the baptism of the Holy Spirit by simply asking God in faith and trust. I believe that there is no way to live in total victory without receiving and understanding the baptism of the Holy Spirit. But I haven't written this book to try to convince anyone. I've done this teaching to be used as a tool to help people who are sincere seekers. It is a catalyst for people who want to receive the baptism of the Holy Spirit and a valuable handbook for those who have already received it and want to have more revelation in this area.

Much of the dissatisfaction that many believers experience in their Christian walk comes from a lack of power in their lives, power which only comes through the infilling of the Holy Spirit. If you are one of those people, I believe that this book can be a turning point in your life.

As we look at this wonderful gift[2] of God called the baptism of the Holy Spirit, I pray that you will approach this subject with an open mind and heart so that you will be able to receive this word clearly and be ministered to and blessed by it in a mighty way.

1
JESUS AND BAPTISM

1
JESUS AND BAPTISM

~

John the Baptist appeared in the wilderness
(desert), preaching a baptism [obligating]
repentance ... in order to obtain forgiveness of
and release from sins. ...

And he preached, saying, After me comes He
Who is stronger (more powerful and more
valiant) than I, the strap of Whose sandals I am
not worthy or fit to stoop down and unloose.

I have baptized you with water, but He will
baptize you with the Holy Spirit.

Mark 1:4,7,8

To baptize means to submerge.[1] We
could say it means to engulf, which may

cause whatever is baptized to be filled with something.

For example, if we took an empty drinking glass and submerged it in water, it would become engulfed and filled with that water. We could say that glass had been baptized in water or baptized with water.

That is a simple explanation of what I believe takes place when we receive the baptism of the Holy Spirit — we become completely engulfed and filled with all the power and presence of God, which means we don't have to go through life trying to do everything on our own anymore.

Jesus didn't try to do His ministry on His Own. First, He was baptized in the Holy Spirit.

Jesus Was Baptized —
in Water and in Spirit

In those days Jesus came from Nazareth of Galilee and was baptized by John in the Jordan.

And when He came up out of the water, at once he [John] saw the heavens torn open and the [Holy] Spirit like a dove coming down [to enter] into Him.

And there came a voice out from within heaven, You are My Beloved Son; in You I am well pleased.

Mark 1:9-11

In this passage we see that Jesus received the baptism of the Holy Spirit at the time of His water baptism.

Some people try to make a doctrine out of that event, saying that everybody receives the baptism of the Holy Spirit at the time they are baptized in water. Others claim that everyone is baptized in the Holy Spirit when they are born again, or when they accept Jesus as their Savior. Still others teach that children receive the baptism of the Holy Spirit at the time of their confirmation or other religious ceremony.

We must be careful not to put God into a doctrinal box. God may do some things in an ordinary way, but He Himself is supernatural and can go far beyond the borders or limits we human beings may try to place on Him.

I know this is true by personal experience because I received the baptism of the Holy Spirit in my car without even knowing what was happening to me or that it had a name. I was a believer in Jesus Christ, so the Holy Spirit was in me, but I knew I was a Christian who had no victory and was looking for a deeper walk with God. As I cried out to God for more, I was baptized in the Spirit right there in my car. That may not be the usual place for God to baptize someone in the Holy Spirit, but God chose to meet me at the point of my need in a rather unusual way.

As another example, I know a woman who did receive the baptism of the Holy

Spirit as a twelve-year-old child at her confirmation but did not know what had happened to her until years later when in middle age she realized what had taken place in her youth. She became aware that this experience was a catalyst for many other powerful things that had happened in her life through the years.

The bottom line is, people can be baptized in the Holy Spirit at the time of their water baptism, just as Jesus was, though that is not always the case. But whenever the Holy Spirit is poured out upon people, He comes upon them to stay with them in a special, powerful way, just as He did with Jesus.

Descend and Remain

*John gave further evidence, saying, I have seen
the Spirit descending as a dove out of heaven,
and it dwelt on Him [never to depart].*

*And I did not know Him nor recognize Him,
but He Who sent me to baptize in (with)
water said to me, Upon Him Whom you shall
see the Spirit descend and remain, that One is
He Who baptizes with the Holy Spirit.*

John 1:32,33

Notice the two phrases used here in this
passage: *never to depart* and *descend and
remain.* Why were they used in reference
to the baptism of the Holy Spirit?

Under the Old Covenant, many times
the Spirit of God would come upon
people temporarily in certain situations

or for certain events. He was with them but not in them.

For example, when the Old Testament prophets prophesied in the name of the Lord, the Spirit of God would come upon them and give them messages for His people.[2] The prophets would then deliver those messages under the anointing, or power, of God and the guidance and leadership of the Holy Spirit. But then the Holy Spirit would leave the prophets and would not come again until God had another message to give them.

It is important for us to know that the Bible says that the Spirit of God descended upon Jesus and remained, never to depart. Thus, we may be assured we are never without the help we need for any task in life.

Jesus as the Baptizer in the Spirit

But you are not living the life of the flesh, you are living the life of the Spirit, if the [Holy] Spirit of God [really] dwells within you [directs and controls you]. But if anyone does not possess the [Holy] Spirit of Christ, he is none of His [he does not belong to Christ, is not truly a child of God].

Romans 8:9

Jesus is the Baptizer in the Holy Spirit.[3] This baptism in the Spirit is not a visitation or a one-time occurrence in the life of the believer.

When Jesus baptizes a person in the Holy Spirit, the Spirit comes into that individual's life to take up permanent residence there. But before a person can be baptized in the Holy Spirit, that person must be born again.

If we have the Spirit of Jesus Christ living in us, then the Holy Spirit is there within us also because the Father, the Son and the Holy Spirit are all One.[4] This is one of those things that our finite mind cannot grasp. It does not work out mathematically, but, nonetheless, it is true. God is a triune God — one God — yet three Persons. We could not even believe in Jesus if it were not for the Holy Spirit Who brings truth and revelation to us. That is part of His ministry.

2
THE MINISTRY OF
THE HOLY SPIRIT

2

THE MINISTRY OF THE HOLY SPIRIT

⤳

And while being in their company and eating at the table with them, He commanded them not to leave Jerusalem but to wait for what the Father had promised, Of which [He said] you have heard Me speak.

For John baptized with water, but not many days from now you shall be baptized with (placed in, introduced into) the Holy Spirit.

Acts 1:4,5

If anyone is born again, the Holy Spirit is definitely working in their life. I always say, "They have the Holy Spirit, but until they are filled completely with the Holy Spirit, He doesn't have them."

The Holy Spirit began to work in my life when, as a nine-year-old child, I went to an altar and asked Jesus to be my Savior. But I lived many, many years as a miserable, unhappy, discontented, unfulfilled, unfruitful Christian who had no victory in my life. Like many Christians, I had enough of Jesus to stay out of hell — but not enough to walk in victory. He was my Savior but not my Lord.

But when I received the baptism of the Holy Spirit, He began a brand-new work in me. A new era in my life was

opened up to me, one in which I saw the
Word of God in an entirely new way.
There was a new love for God and His
Word in my heart that drew me to want
to know Him like I had never known
Him before. As a result of the ministry
of the Holy Spirit within me, I was able
to start winning the victory over my
problems, which were many.

It is a vital part of the ministry of the
Holy Spirit to help us and strengthen us
so we can have real victory in our life
and enjoy the abundant life that Christ
died to provide for us. The baptism of
the Holy Spirit is such an important part
of our life as believers that in Acts 1 Jesus
commanded His disciples not to leave
Jerusalem right away after His ascension

into heaven, but to wait for the promise of the Father, which was the baptism of the Holy Spirit.

Some of the other various roles and functions of the Holy Spirit in our life are:

He prompts us to pray and teaches us how to pray.

He strengthens us in our time of need.

He alone can minister to our inner man when we are hurting.

The Holy Spirit also prompts us to make correct choices, but He will *never* force us to make them. He must be *allowed* to be in charge. We cannot change the things in our life that need to be changed, but the Holy Spirit can.

The Holy Spirit Remains with Us Forever

*And I will ask the Father, and He will give
you another Comforter (Counselor, Helper,
Intercessor, Advocate, Strengthener, and
Standby), that He may remain with you
forever —*

*The Spirit of Truth, Whom the world cannot
receive (welcome, take to its heart), because it
does not see Him or know and recognize Him.
But you know and recognize Him, for He lives
with you [constantly] and will be in you.*

John 14:16,17

Here in John 14, and later in John 15
and 16, Jesus makes reference to the
Holy Spirit and His ministry among
believers — and that ministry has not
changed. It is important to understand
His ministry so we can appreciate it and
cooperate with it.

The present-day ministry of the Holy Spirit is so powerful and so precious. Since we are believers in Jesus Christ, He is already in us and with us, but He wants to come and dwell in us fully and completely.

First Corinthians 6:19 tells us that we are the temple of the Holy Spirit. We are His house. The Spirit wants to indwell the entire house and not just one room or a portion of it.

As Jesus told His disciples, the Holy Spirit wants to come and take up residence within us for a purpose. Remember that He wants to comfort us, counsel us, intercede for us and pray through us, be our Advocate or Lawyer, strengthen us, and stand by us and help us in everything we face or go through in this life. And as we saw when He descended upon Jesus at His baptism, the Holy Spirit wants to come and remain with us forever.

That was a key issue for the disciples because they were used to the Holy Spirit coming upon them in certain situations and then leaving when that situation was over.

For example, in the tenth chapter of Luke, we read how these same disciples received a mighty anointing of the Holy Spirit when Jesus sent them out two by two into all the surrounding towns to minister in His name. He told them to preach the Gospel, cast out devils and lay hands on the sick. They came back tremendously excited because even the demons were subject to them in Jesus' name. Jesus explained to them that He had given them authority and power over all the power of the enemy. In other words, the demons were subject to the disciples through the anointing and the power of the Holy Spirit that was upon them.

Then in John chapters 14, 15 and 16, Jesus told His disciples something different. He referred to the time when the Father would send the Holy Spirit upon them to remain with them forever.

It was not as though the disciples knew nothing of the Holy Spirit. As Jesus was telling them, they would know and recognize the Spirit when He came because He (Jesus) had been with them. The good news was that now He would *always* be with them through the Holy Spirit to work His ministry in them forever.

And that same promise is made to you and me today.

The Holy Spirit as Teacher and Guide

But the Comforter (Counselor, Helper, Intercessor, Advocate, Strengthener, Standby), the Holy Spirit, Whom the Father will send in My name [in My place, to represent Me and act on My behalf], He will teach you all things. And He will cause you to recall (will remind you of, bring to your remembrance) everything I have told you.

John 14:26

It is the Holy Spirit Who teaches us. He is also the One Who causes us to remember what we are taught.

In John 16:12 Jesus told the disciples, *I have still many things to say to you, but you are not able to bear them or to take them upon you or to grasp them now.*

Then in the next verse He went on to say, *But when He, the Spirit of Truth (the Truth-giving Spirit) comes, He will guide you into all the Truth (the whole, full Truth). For He will not speak His own message [on His own authority]; but He will tell whatever He hears [from the Father; He will give the message that has been given to Him], and He will announce and declare to you the things that are to come [that will happen in the future].*

Finally, in verse 14, Jesus said to them about the Holy Spirit, *He will honor and glorify Me, because He will take of (receive, draw upon) what is Mine and will reveal (declare, disclose, transmit) it to you.*

What wonderful promises from God. They let us know that we can be led and guided by the Holy Spirit within us and not by outside forces. If we will listen to the Holy Spirit by following our heart instead of listening to the enemy Satan, or following our head or our feelings, the Holy Spirit will reveal God's will for us in every situation.

The Holy Spirit as a Witness for Jesus

But when the Comforter (Counselor, Helper, Advocate, Intercessor, Strengthener, Standby) comes, Whom I will send to you from the

*Father, the Spirit of Truth Who comes
(proceeds) from the Father, He [Himself] will
testify regarding Me.*

John 15:26

In this passage, Jesus tells His disciples
that one important part of the ministry
of the Holy Spirit is to act as a witness
for Him.

In verse 27 Jesus follows that statement
by adding, *But you also will testify and
be My witnesses, because you have been
with Me from the beginning.*

That applies to us as much as it did to
the first disciples. As followers of Jesus
Christ, we are also called to be witnesses
for Him. We can be ever ready to
fulfill our responsibilities as believers,
empowered by the Holy Spirit.

The Holy Spirit as
Representative of Jesus

*However, I am telling you nothing but the
truth when I say it is profitable (good,
expedient, advantageous) for you that I go
away. Because if I do not go away, the
Comforter (Counselor, Helper, Advocate,
Intercessor, Strengthener, Standby) will not
come to you [into close fellowship with you];
but if I go away, I will send Him to you [to be
in close fellowship with you].*

John 16:7

Just before the Crucifixion, Jesus told
His disciples that He was about to leave
them, and they were filled with sorrow.
But He went on to tell them that unless
He left them and went away, the Holy
Spirit would not come to be with them

in close and continual fellowship, which would be much better for them.

Now you may be thinking, "But how could anything be better than having Jesus right here with us?"

Jesus was in a human body just as you and I are. As one Person, He could only be in one place at a time.

But the Holy Spirit, Who comes in Jesus' name to represent Him to every believer, can indwell each of us fully at the same time all over the entire world. This is another one of those things that our carnal minds cannot understand, yet it is true. The Holy Spirit not only indwells us with His precious Presence, but also the presence of the Father and the Son.[1]

The Holy Spirit as Sanctifier

The Holy Spirit also reveals to each of us the will of God for us individually, and He works God's will in us, which includes the process of sanctification. This is another part of the Holy Spirit's job — to make us sanctified.[2] The word *sanctification* simply refers to the process that God uses to do a work in us by His indwelling Holy Spirit to make us more and more holy until finally we become just like His Son Jesus. This process is lifelong and will be completely perfected when Jesus returns.[3]

The Holy Spirit is called "holy" because that is what He is, and His purpose in taking up residence in us is to make us holy too. He is the Sanctifier, the agent of sanctification in our life. If you study the subject of holiness, you will learn that there is no such thing as a person becoming holy apart from a great involvement with the Holy Spirit in their life. Why? Because the Holy Spirit is the power of God given to us to do in us and through us and for us and to us what we could never do on our own. We cannot make ourselves holy, but the Holy Spirit can.

3
EMPOWERED BY THE HOLY SPIRIT

3

EMPOWERED BY
THE HOLY SPIRIT

But you shall receive power (ability, efficiency, and might) when the Holy Spirit has come upon you, and you shall be My witnesses in Jerusalem and all Judea and Samaria and to the ends (the very bounds) of the earth.

And when He had said this, even as they were looking [at Him], He was caught up, and a cloud received and carried Him away out of their sight.

Acts 1:8,9

Power is something everyone seeks in one form or another. God's will is for His children to have power. But many

people who are not in right relationship
with Him seek power in wrong ways —
through exercising power over people,
excessive power in the business world,
receiving a promotion, etc.

Some believers don't have any idea
that they are supposed to be powerful,
and they are "weakness-minded," which
causes them to be filled with an "I can't"
mentality. Recognizing that we have
godly power helps us get rid of the "I
can't" attitude.

After we receive the baptism of the
Holy Spirit, we get filled with "can do."
We are no longer unable — we are able.
We are no longer weak, but we are
mighty. The truth is that nothing is too

hard for a believer who is baptized in the Holy Spirit and has the power of God in their life.

In the passage in Acts 1:8, the Greek word for the word *power* is *dunamis,* which means, ". . . miracle(s), power, strength. . . ."[1] This is a special miracle-working power. Jesus told us we could receive "dunamis" power through the infilling of the Holy Spirit.

Waiting for the Promise

Just before Jesus ascended into heaven, He told His disciples that they were to wait for what the Father had promised, the baptism of the Holy Spirit, which the disciples would soon receive. Why did He want them to wait for it?

Nelson's Illustrated Bible Dictionary defines *power* as, "The ability or strength to perform an activity or deed. . . ."[2] Remember, the Holy Spirit is the power of Almighty God, and He empowers us to reach and accomplish things that go beyond human limitations. The disciples received the baptism of the Holy Spirit, which enabled them to be witnesses for the Lord throughout the known world.

God desires every believer to be witnesses in our world, but He doesn't expect us to do it in our own strength and ability. When He calls us to do something, He equips us to do it through the power of the Holy Spirit.

Are you a Christian who has power, ability, efficiency and might? Do you have enough of the power of the Holy Spirit flowing in your life that your life is changing and your problems are being overcome by the Word of God and the power of His Spirit? Are you making a difference in someone else's life? If you answered no, then you need to receive the baptism of the Holy Spirit; it will change you from *doing* witnessing to *being* a witness for the Lord.

Before I received the baptism of the Holy Spirit, I was out witnessing to others. I was part of an evangelism team that went door to door weekly telling others about Jesus. But although I was *doing* witnessing, I was not *being* a witness. The reason was that although I was born again and had the Holy Spirit in me and working in my life as a Christian, I did not have enough of the power of God flowing in my own personal day-to-day life to cause me to be like Jesus.

Now I'm not saying that we cannot do anything at all for God without the baptism of the Holy Spirit. I believe that God's anointing can come upon us to accomplish and do different things. But for me it was like having a little trickle versus a flood. And with the kind of problems I had in my life, I needed more than a trickle; I needed a flood. I had been sexually, mentally and emotionally abused in my childhood, and the negative results were very prominent in my life and personality.

At the time of Jesus' ascension into heaven, He wanted the disciples to be flooded with God's power, or the fullness of God, in their lives. No one could be born again until Jesus died on the cross and rose from the dead. He is called *. . . the firstborn among many brethren.*[3] After His resurrection from the dead, He had appeared to the disciples and breathed upon them saying, . . . *Receive the Holy Spirit!*[4] I believe the disciples were born again at that time. Jesus had been born again from the dead, and now others could share in His victory.

God had originally created man to be spiritually alive. Our spirit was to be filled with the Spirit of God and be the leader of our body and soul.[5] When Adam and Eve disobeyed God and sinned in the Garden of Eden, they didn't die physically but spiritually, and they began to live in the soulish realm.[6] When a person is born again, their spirit is filled with the life of God.

Before we receive the baptism of the Holy Spirit, our soul runs our life. When we are born again, the Holy Spirit is in the depths of our spirit man, desiring and seeking to run our life, but He can only do that when we give Him permission to come and *fill us*.

Although the disciples had become born again and *received* the Spirit, and they had a measure of the Holy Spirit, they had not yet received the promise of the Father and been totally *filled* with the Spirit.

If they had received the promise of the Father at that point, they wouldn't have been waiting for it in Acts Chapter 2. That total infilling was to take place later, after the ascension of Jesus, on the Day of Pentecost.

The Promise Fulfilled

And when the day of Pentecost had fully come, they were all assembled together in one place,

When suddenly there came a sound from heaven like the rushing of a violent tempest blast, and it filled the whole house in which they were sitting.

And there appeared to them tongues resembling fire, which were separated and distributed and which settled on each one of them.

And they were all filled (diffused throughout their souls) with the Holy Spirit and began to speak in other (different, foreign) languages (tongues), as the Spirit kept giving them clear and loud expression [in each tongue in appropriate words].

Acts 2:1-4

Ever since the ascension of Jesus, the disciples had been waiting for the promise of the Father, which Jesus had told them about. On the Day of Pentecost, that promise was fulfilled when the Holy Spirit was poured out upon them as they were all assembled together in one place.

What was the immediate result of this outpouring and infilling of the Holy Spirit? The disciples were given the ability to speak in tongues, in foreign languages they had not learned.

The Gift of Tongues

Now there were then residing in Jerusalem Jews, devout and God-fearing men from every country under heaven.

And when this sound was heard, the multitude came together and they were astonished and bewildered, because each one heard them [the apostles] speaking in his own [particular] dialect.

And they were beside themselves with amazement, saying, Are not all these who are talking Galileans?

Then how is it that we hear, each of us, in our own (particular) dialect to which we were born?

Acts 2:5-8

When the disciples began to speak in tongues at Pentecost, it was in languages that they did not understand, but others did.

Later, in 1 Corinthians 13:1, the apostle Paul writes, *If I [can] speak in the tongues of men and [even] of angels, but have not love . . ., I am only a noisy gong or a clanging cymbal.*

So apparently it is possible to speak in "the tongues of men," meaning languages known to other people but not known to the speaker. It is also possible to speak in "the tongues of angels," or languages that are known only by God and which no one, not even the one doing the speaking, can understand unless the Lord gives the interpretation.

The basic message of this chapter is the power, efficiency, ability and might that is made available to believers by the infilling of the Holy Spirit. We will examine the subject of tongues and the interpretation of tongues in more detail in a later chapter, but it was mentioned here because it is one of the manifestations of the outpouring of the Holy Spirit.

The Outpouring of the Spirit

And it shall come to pass in the last days, God declares, that I will pour out of My Spirit upon all mankind, and your sons and your daughters shall prophesy [telling forth the divine counsels] and your young men shall see visions (divinely granted appearances), and your old men shall dream [divinely suggested] dreams.

Yes, and on My menservants also and on My maidservants in those days I will pour out of My Spirit, and they shall prophesy [telling forth the divine counsels and predicting future events pertaining especially to God's kingdom].

And I will show wonders in the sky above and signs on the earth beneath. . . .

Acts 2:17-19

This passage, a reference to Joel 2:28-30, is what Jesus was referring to when He spoke of the promise of the Father. He was saying that the time had come for this Old Testament prophecy to be fulfilled, and it was on the Day of Pentecost.

Since that day when the Holy Spirit was first poured out upon God's people, the Lord has been showing forth greater signs and wonders through believers. As we read in Mark 16:20, after Jesus ascended into heaven, His disciples . . . *went out and preached everywhere, while the Lord kept working with them and confirming the message by the attesting signs and miracles that closely accompanied [it].*

He is still doing that in our day. Throughout history there have been different outpourings of the Spirit like the one prophesied in Joel Chapter 2. Particularly since 1900,[7] God has been pouring out His Spirit upon all those who will open up their hearts to Him and receive a new move of His Spirit in their lives through the empowering of the Holy Spirit.

Let's look at how the Spirit moved in the disciples' lives when they were empowered by the Holy Spirit on the Day of Pentecost.

The Empowerment of the Disciples

For the promise [of the Holy Spirit] is to and for you and your children, and to and for all that are far away, [even] to and for as many as the Lord our God invites and bids to come to Himself.

Acts 2:39

When the multitude heard the disciples
speaking about the wonders of God,
each in their own native language, they
were . . . *beside themselves with amazement
and were puzzled and bewildered, saying
one to another, What can this mean?*[8]

Some of them, however, were not
impressed, claiming that the disciples
were just full of too much wine.

But Peter, empowered by the Holy
Spirit, stood up before the crowd and
preached to them, telling them in verses
14 through 16,

> . . . *You Jews and all you residents of Jerusalem,
> let this be [explained] to you so that you will
> know and understand; listen closely to what I
> have to say.*

For these men are not drunk, as you imagine, for it is [only] the third hour (about 9:00 A.M.) of the day;

But [instead] this is [the beginning of] what was spoken through the prophet Joel.

Then, full of the power of the Spirit, Peter went on to explain to the gathered Jews that Jesus, Whom they had crucified, was the long-awaited Messiah sent to save the world from its sin.

When the multitude heard this, they were cut to the heart and asked Peter and the other disciples what they should do.

In Acts 2:38 Peter answered them, *Repent (change your views and purpose to accept the will of God in your inner selves instead of rejecting it) and be baptized, every one of you, in the name of Jesus*

Christ for the forgiveness of and release from your sins; and you shall receive the gift of the Holy Spirit.

What Peter was telling these people was that they needed to repent, be born again and receive the outpouring of the Holy Spirit to empower them to live the Christian life.

We believers do not have to live a powerless life. We are to live as Christ lived — empowered by the Holy Spirit. *The empowering of the Holy Spirit is part of our spiritual inheritance as sons and daughters of God.*[9]

4
"GOD, THERE HAS GOT TO BE MORE!"

4
"GOD, THERE HAS GOT TO BE MORE!"

I assure you, most solemnly I tell you, We speak only of what we know [we know absolutely what we are talking about]; we have actually seen what we are testifying to [we were eyewitnesses of it]. . . .

John 3:11

In this chapter I would like to share with you my testimony of how I received the baptism of the Holy Spirit and what it has meant in my own life.

I came from a very rough background in which I was abused verbally, mentally, emotionally, physically and sexually. So although I was born again at the age of nine, by the time I became a grown woman, I still had problems because I had brought the effects of my childhood abuse forward into my adult life.

The reason I had never manifested any of the fruit of the Spirit in my life was that I had never received any teaching of the Word of God. But through all this time the Lord was with me attempting to lead and guide me the best I would let Him. I believe He kept me out of a lot of trouble that I would have gotten into had He not been protecting me.

When I married Dave Meyer, he was born again, baptized in the Spirit and loved God with all of his heart. But although he had been baptized in the Holy Spirit, he never talked to me about this marvelous experience. He didn't speak in tongues either because he knew nothing about it. But he was definitely full of the power of the Holy Spirit.

Dave did not even know that what he had experienced had a name, that it was called the baptism of the Holy Spirit. All he knew was that God had met him in a very special way at a time when he was crying out to the Lord for more power in his life. God did meet him, and he was transformed into a more powerful Christian from that point on.

This occurred when Dave was about eighteen years old, and I met him when he was twenty-six. I used to say that God baptized Dave in the Holy Spirit and gave him a few years to walk in it and receive instructions from the Lord to equip him to be able to handle me because I was a woman with problems.

Because I was so troubled, the Lord had to send me a Christian husband, one who was able to walk in love with me although I was not being very lovely.

On the Way to Work

. . . I have appeared to you for this purpose, that I might appoint you to serve as [My] minister and to bear witness both to what you have seen of Me and to that in which I will appear to you.

Acts 26:16

After we got married, Dave asked me to go to church with him, and I agreed. Somehow I knew I needed to go to church and have a closer walk with God. I had so many problems in my life that I needed someone to literally take my hand and lead me.

So I started going to church with Dave, and I began to get closer to the Lord because I was in the Word, and I really loved God. I was born again, but I was still a weak, powerless Christian with many problems I didn't know how to overcome.

After Dave and I had been married for about ten years, I was on my way to work one day totally fed up with myself and the way I was acting and aggravated because I had no power to overcome anything.

As I drove along, I was talking to the Lord about it and said, "God, there has got to be more. There must be something I am missing because I see in Your Word that people lived in victory, and I certainly don't have any victory."

To my utter astonishment and amazement, God spoke to me in something like an audible voice. I was not accustomed to that kind of thing happening, but if God speaks to you, you certainly know it's God. I knew what He said to me was God because it was

something that had been in my heart
that only He knew.

I was so excited that God had spoken
to me that when I got to work, I called
Dave and told him, "You won't believe it,
but God spoke to me in the car this
morning!" Dave could tell I was excited,
and just my excitement alone convinced
him that God had indeed spoken to me.

After that, I moved into a realm of
faith that was uncommon for me. I just
absolutely knew that God was going to
do something in my life, but I didn't
have the slightest idea what it was. Yet I
had such rest and peace in my mind and
heart that it really didn't matter to me
what God did or when He did it. I just

knew that He was in control in a way that I had never known before.

That was on a Friday, and I always got my hair done on Friday. Then Dave and I always went out bowling that night.

I was on my way home in the car and had just turned onto an exit road that led to our house. I was waiting for a traffic light to change when all of a sudden I was engulfed by the Holy Ghost. It felt like someone had opened me up and poured a whole bucket of liquid love into me.

When God begins to move in your life, He starts moving from all directions, and from that moment on, I have been radically different. I had peace. I had a new love in my heart for everyone, even those whom I could not stand previously. I would drive down the road and even the weeds along the highway would look beautiful to me. I was entirely changed and transformed.

People began to say to me, "Joyce, what has happened to you? Something is different about you."

I realized that God had done something special for me, but I still didn't know what to call it.

A New Language

And these attesting signs will accompany those who believe: in My name . . . they will speak in new languages.

Mark 16:17

The Lord began to lead me to turn on the radio when I came home from work at night, something I had never done before. I found a Christian radio station that had a program called "Testimony Time." As I listened to people give testimonies about being baptized in the Holy Spirit, I began to realize that was what had happened to me. They talked about speaking in tongues, but I didn't know anything about that. However, they did recommend some books to read.

One of the first books I read was by Pat Boone called *A New Song*.[1] In this book, he described his experience with the baptism of the Holy Spirit and how he had received the gift of speaking in tongues. As I read that testimony, faith rose up in me to open my mouth and try to cooperate with the Holy Spirit by speaking in tongues.

At that time I received only four words, and it didn't take the devil long to convince me that I had made them up. So for two or three weeks I didn't know what to do. I kept asking God to give me the gift of tongues, which He had already done, but I didn't know it.

Later, I was helping one of my children with a project, and I looked up something in the dictionary. When I did, I discovered that this dictionary contained some Latin words that I thought looked like some of the words I felt I received when I was asking God to give me the gift of tongues. As I continued to look up the others, I discovered that all four of them meant something like "Omnipotent heavenly Father."

Once God gave me that confirmation, I knew for sure that I had received them from God and that there was no way I could have made them up, and I began to try to exercise the gift of tongues. Suddenly one day as I was going to work, I received a whole language from God. I pulled the car off the road and sat there and wept, praying in tongues.

Everyone's Experience Is Different

But to each one is given the manifestation of the [Holy] Spirit [the evidence, the spiritual illumination of the Spirit] for good and profit.

1 Corinthians 12:7

I thought it was important to share my whole experience with you because many people speak in tongues as soon as they are baptized in the Holy Spirit, but others speak in tongues later, as I did.

The main thing is to realize that not everyone's experience is the same. None of us are going to have exactly the same experience the disciples had at Pentecost when there was such a mighty outpouring of the Holy Spirit. God is still doing mighty things today, though not necessarily the same way He did back then in that manifestation.

Just remember that you are an individual, and God has an individual plan for you that will be manifested if you will continue to seek Him for it.

5
SEEKING THE BAPTISM OF THE HOLY SPIRIT

5

SEEKING THE BAPTISM OF THE HOLY SPIRIT

~

. . . whoever would come near to God must
[necessarily] believe that God exists and that
He is the rewarder of those who earnestly and
diligently seek Him [out].

Hebrews 11:6

I believe the baptism of the Holy Spirit
is for sincere seekers.

So often people just want to *try* spiritual
things without being serious about
seeking after them. For example, they will
get into a prayer line and let someone pray
for them to receive the baptism of the

Holy Spirit with a half-hearted attitude of, "I'll try that and see if it works."

God knows when a person is serious about seeking Him, and I must emphasize the word *serious*.

As I mentioned earlier, I was baptized in the Holy Spirit without even knowing there was such a thing. All I knew was that there had to be more to the Christian life than what I was experiencing, and I wanted to have it, so I cried out to God for it. I believe I received the baptism of the Holy Spirit because I was serious about wanting more of God so I could live a holy, victorious life.

If you want to receive the baptism of the Holy Spirit, I think one of the questions you need to ask yourself is, "*Why* do I want to be baptized in the Holy Spirit?"

The baptism of the Holy Spirit is not just for goose bumps. It should not be sought just for the gifts of the Holy Spirit that go with it, such as speaking in tongues.

I believe the baptism of the Holy Spirit is for those believers who really want to live holy lives, those who want the fullness of God within them because they truly want the power and ability to do God's will.

Timing

To everything there is a season, and a time for every matter or purpose under heaven.

Ecclesiastes 3:1

Can you receive the baptism of the Holy Spirit anytime you are ready?

The answer is yes and no. I don't mean for that to be a confusing answer, but it depends upon your motives. Are you ready to allow Him to lead and guide you and be the controlling influence in your life?

If so, then you may be ready to receive, but you must be aware that the Holy Spirit is given for a purpose — to get fully involved in your life and work in it to lead you down the good path God has planned for you.

About three weeks after I was baptized in the Holy Spirit, I was called into ministry. I did not know that was going to happen when I sought the fullness of the Lord. I only knew I needed more of God to be able to do whatever it was He had for me to accomplish in my life.

The same is true for you. You may not know yet what God is calling and preparing you for, but you must remember that whatever His plan is for you, the baptism of the Holy Spirit is an equipping for it. It may not be full-time ministry, but we are all called to do something wonderful for God.

Jesus told His disciples that they would be baptized in the Holy Spirit in order to be His witnesses. God wants to give you the power to be something. Are you ready to receive that gift and become what He wants you to be?

The Baptism of Fire

John answered them all by saying, I baptize you with water; but He Who is mightier than I is coming, the strap of Whose sandals I am not fit to unfasten. He will baptize you with the Holy Spirit and with fire.

Luke 3:16

Many people want the baptism of the Holy Spirit, but they don't want the baptism of fire.

What is the baptism of fire? Condensed to its simplest form, it is allowing the Holy Spirit to work in our life to bring us out of carnality and into new levels of holiness all the time.

In other words, it is the crucifixion of the flesh; it is spiritual maturity.

In Galatians 2:20, the apostle Paul described this crucifixion of the flesh when he wrote, *I have been crucified with Christ [in Him I have shared His crucifixion]; it is no longer I who live, but Christ (the Messiah) lives in me; and the life I now live in the body I live by faith in (by adherence to and reliance on and complete trust in) the Son of God, Who loved me and gave Himself up for me.*

As He floods your life, the Holy Spirit wants to move in and permeate every area. He wants to live in every room of your heart. Before He can do that, you must be willing to move out.

This is all part of the process of sanctification that we mentioned earlier, which is one of the ministries of the Holy Spirit in the life of the believer. The Bible speaks of it as being transformed into the image of God from glory to glory: *But we all, with open face beholding as in a glass the glory of the Lord, are changed into the same image from glory to glory, even as by the Spirit of the Lord.*[1]

There is a work to be done in the life of each one of us. We are in the process of a progressive change and growth brought about within us by the Holy Spirit, Who wants to fill us totally with His marvelous Presence and power.

If you are ready to receive the fullness of the Holy Spirit in your life, what should you do? The answer is really very simple.

Ask and Continue to Ask

If you then, evil as you are, know how to give good gifts [gifts that are to their advantage] to your children, how much more will your heavenly Father give the Holy Spirit to those who ask and continue to ask Him!

Luke 11:13

In my meetings, I use this verse simply as a catalyst to say to people, "If you want to receive the baptism of the Holy Spirit, then ask God for it."

According to this passage, God has promised to give the Holy Spirit to all those who ask.

When you ask, how will He lead you to receive? He may lead you sovereignly, as He did with me and also my husband.

Dave was baptized in the Holy Spirit at the age of eighteen while he was in the bathroom. Dave was just thoroughly disgusted with his behavior and knew he did not have the power to change himself. So in desperation he prayed to the Lord, "God, I am not leaving this bathroom until You do something in my life. I don't know what it is that You need to do, but I am not leaving here until You do it."

Not only was Dave baptized in the Holy Spirit, but he also received a physical healing in his eyes.

So God may move upon you in an unusual way — in a car or in a room of your house or while you are out taking a walk. He may pour out His Spirit upon you when someone else lays hands on you in prayer. That may be in a meeting in which someone is ministering the baptism of the Holy Spirit, or it may be at your church or in your pastor's study or even in the home of a friend.

Whatever the circumstances, just open your heart to the Lord in faith and allow Him to give you all that He has available for you. This wonderful Gift of God called the Holy Spirit is the One Who brings to you and me every other good gift. He has been given to us to bring forth into our life everything that we need.

6

THE GIFTS OF
THE HOLY SPIRIT

6

THE GIFTS OF
THE HOLY SPIRIT

⌒

*Now about the spiritual gifts (the special
endowments of supernatural energy),
brethren, I do not want you to be misinformed.*

1 Corinthians 12:1

I attended church for many years and
never heard one sermon or lesson of any
kind on the gifts of the Spirit. I did not
know what they were, let alone that they
were available to me.

Many people are afraid of receiving
the Holy Spirit because they don't
understand either the Holy Spirit or the

gifts of the Spirit. For that reason, I would like to share with you some important Scriptures on this subject.

In 1 Corinthians the apostle Paul wrote to the church that he had established in the city of Corinth to explain to those new believers something about the nature, operation and purpose of the gifts that the Holy Spirit bestows upon people.

In 1 Corinthians 12 he begins by telling the Corinthian believers that he does not want them to be ignorant of these things. Then he goes on to explain the gifts to them.

A Variety of Spiritual Gifts

Now there are distinctive varieties and distributions of endowments (gifts, extraordinary powers distinguishing certain Christians, due to the power of divine grace operating in their souls by the Holy Spirit) and they vary, but the [Holy] Spirit remains the same.

And there are distinctive varieties of service and ministration, but it is the same Lord [Who is served].

And there are distinctive varieties of operation [of working to accomplish things], but it is the same God Who inspires and energizes them all in all.

1 Corinthians 12:4-6

Paul tells the Corinthians that there is a variety of spiritual gifts and that they are distributed to different people in the church according to the will and purpose of God.

Although the spiritual gifts are distinct one from the other and operate differently to accomplish different purposes, they are all under the direction of God, Who gives them life and energy.

The Gifts Defined

But to each one is given the manifestation of the [Holy] Spirit [the evidence, the spiritual illumination of the Spirit] for good and profit.

To one is given in and through the [Holy] Spirit [the power to speak] a message of wisdom, and to another [the power to express] a word of knowledge and understanding according to the same [Holy] Spirit;

To another [wonder-working] faith by the same [Holy] Spirit, to another the extraordinary powers of healing by the one Spirit;

To another the working of miracles, to another prophetic insight (the gift of interpreting the divine will and purpose); to another the ability to discern and distinguish between [the utterances of true] spirits [and false ones], to another various kinds of [unknown] tongues, to another the ability to interpret [such] tongues.

All these [gifts, achievements, abilities] are inspired and brought to pass by one and the same [Holy] Spirit, Who apportions to each person individually [exactly] as He chooses.

1 Corinthians 12:7-11

So we see that when God gives the Holy Spirit to those who ask Him, the Holy Spirit distributes among them different spiritual gifts to be used for different purposes.

Generally, these gifts are known by the description of them found in the *King*

James Version of this passage: word of wisdom, word of knowledge, faith, healing, working of miracles, prophecy, discerning of spirits, tongues and interpretation of tongues.

Remember, the gifts vary, but they are all from the same Holy Spirit.

The *word of wisdom* is a form of spiritual guidance that lets an individual know supernaturally by the Holy Spirit how to handle a certain issue in a way that is beyond their natural learning or experience and lines up with God's purpose.[1]

The *word of knowledge* operates much the same way as the word of wisdom. There are a number of different interpretations of the word of knowledge, but the one believers generally follow is this: We find it valuable because suddenly an individual knows something that God reveals to them about their life or about what He is doing in another person's life that there is no natural way for them to know.[2]

I believe there are certain individuals to whom God gives the *gift of faith* for specific occasions such as a dangerous missionary trip or a very challenging situation. When this gift is operating in people, they are able to comfortably believe God in or for something that other people would see as impossible.[3]

The *gifts of healing* work with the gift of faith. Although every believer is encouraged to lay hands on the sick, pray and see them recover,[4] God may choose to use certain individuals in a special healing ministry.[5] In other words, as believers, we can always pray for the sick, but the gifts of healing may not always be present, just as the gift of faith may not always be present. We can always pray in faith, using the measure of faith that the Bible tells us God has given to every person,[6] but the supernatural endowment of faith is given as the Spirit wills.

Miracles are things that cannot be explained, things that do not occur through ordinary means. We all can and should believe God for miracles in our lives, but God will choose certain individuals to have the gift of the *working of miracles* flow through them. It is up to the wisdom of the Holy Spirit whether it occurs once or a few times or on a regular basis.

Prophecy concerns the will of God, and while it is instructive or edifying, sometimes it may bring correction. One may prophesy to another individual or to an entire congregation of people. Sometimes the prophecy is more general; at other times it is very specific. It may come through a prepared message or sermon, or it may come by divine revelation.[7]

Some people say that the *discerning of spirits* gives people supernatural insight into the spirit realm when God allows. They believe that it is not exclusively the discerning of evil or demon spirits[8] but also of divine spirits.[9] Other people believe that discerning of spirits also helps us know the true nature of who we are dealing with, whether they are good or evil,[10] and what the motivation is behind a person or situation.[11] In other words, it involves following our heart and not our head.

These are all abilities, gifts, achievements and endowments of God's supernatural power by which we believers are enabled to accomplish something beyond the ordinary. We experience this power as we use our gifts.

Speaking in tongues and *interpretation of tongues* are part of these nine gifts. The best and easiest way to describe tongues is to say it is a spiritual language, one the Holy Spirit knows and chooses to speak through us but one we do not know. It is the Holy Spirit speaking directly to God through us. We do not understand it with our minds. It is a spiritual thing.

Since all nine of these spiritual gifts are given individually by the Holy Spirit to different people, this question almost always arises: "What if I am baptized in the Holy Spirit, but I am not given the gift of speaking in tongues?"

Speaking in tongues is probably one of the most misunderstood of all the nine gifts of the Spirit, so although we have already mentioned it, we are going to take a closer look at it in the next chapter.

7

IS SPEAKING IN
TONGUES FOR TODAY?

7

IS SPEAKING IN
TONGUES FOR TODAY?

⌇

*And they were all filled (diffused throughout
their souls) with the Holy Spirit and began to
speak in other (different, foreign) languages
(tongues), as the Spirit kept giving them clear
and loud expression [in each tongue in
appropriate words].*

Acts 2:4

In an earlier chapter, we saw that the
Holy Spirit was first poured out upon
believers on the Day of Pentecost when
the disciples were all gathered together,
waiting for the gift that Jesus reminded
them God the Father had promised them.

It is important to note that when the gift of the Holy Spirit was given to the assembled disciples, all 120 of them began to speak in tongues. That gift of speaking in tongues has never been revoked; it is still available to all believers who will receive it today. As we have seen, it is part of the whole range of gifts that are given us through the baptism of the Holy Spirit.

Does Everyone Have All of the Gifts?

Now you [collectively] are Christ's body and [individually] you are members of it, each part severally and distinct [each with his own place and function].

So God has appointed some in the church [for His own use]: first apostles (special messengers); second prophets (inspired

preachers and expounders); third teachers;
then wonder-workers; then those with ability
to heal the sick; helpers; administrators;
[speakers in] different (unknown) tongues.

Are all apostles (special messengers)? Are all
prophets (inspired interpreters of the will and
purposes of God)? Are all teachers? Do all
have the power of performing miracles?

Do all possess extraordinary powers of healing?
Do all speak with tongues? Do all interpret?

1 Corinthians 12:27-30

The obvious answer to all these
questions is no. What Paul is saying here
is that not everyone operates in these
gifts — in the church. However, that
does not mean that not everyone will
receive any one particular gift.

Since that may be confusing, let me explain by giving an example. Not everyone has the gift of healing in the sense that they launch into a full-time ministry of healing people. But, remember, every believer does have the power within them to lay hands on the sick and believe they will recover, as Jesus taught in Mark 16:17,18: *And these attesting signs will accompany those who believe: in My name they will drive out demons; they will speak in new languages; . . . they will lay their hands on the sick, and they will get well.*

Are you a believer? If so, Jesus plainly says in this passage that one of the signs that will accompany you is that you will have the power to drive out demons, speak in tongues and lay hands on the sick and they will recover. That is part of the universal faith in which all of us as believers are empowered to operate in, in our everyday lives.

In James 5:14,15 we are told that we can anoint the sick with oil and pray the prayer of faith over them, and they will be restored to health.

So you and I do not need a special gift from the Holy Spirit to exercise our faith to lay hands on the sick. The same is true of speaking in tongues.

Not everyone has the gift of tongues — to stand up in a congregation and speak in tongues with interpretation, which would equal a prophecy given in the church or worship service. But every believer who receives the baptism of the Holy Spirit has been given the ability to pray in tongues and to speak to God in our own individual prayer language.

Differences in Tongues

For one who speaks in an [unknown] tongue speaks not to men but to God, for no one understands or catches his meaning, because in the [Holy] Spirit he utters secret truths and hidden things [not obvious to the understanding].

But [on the other hand], the one who prophesies [who interprets the divine will and purpose in inspired preaching and teaching] speaks to men for their upbuilding and constructive spiritual progress and encouragement and consolation.

1 Corinthians 14:2,3

In the study Bible compiled by well-respected Bible teacher and scholar Finis Jennings Dake, there is a note on Acts 2:1-8, which is the account of the disciples speaking in tongues on the Day of Pentecost. Of this incident Dake writes:

"This [the speaking in tongues] was similar to the Spirit speaking through the prophets in their own language . . . only here it was with different languages."[1]

In other words, just as God can speak to us through prophets who are speaking in our own language or a language we can understand, He can also speak to us in unknown languages or languages we do not understand and which have to be interpreted for our benefit.

Dake continues, "Though speaking in tongues is done through immediate inspiration by new recipients [of the Holy Spirit] when one has thus received the gift [of speaking in tongues], it then becomes a part of his mental make-up so that he can, if he desires to do so, exercise it without direct inspiration. . . ."[2]

That is, although we may speak in tongues by inspiration of the Holy Spirit at the time we receive the baptism of the Holy Spirit, that does not mean we cannot continue to speak in tongues on our own whenever we choose to do so, such as when we pray.

The reason I included this note from Dake is that many people who speak in tongues at the moment they receive the baptism of the Holy Spirit think they can never exercise that particular gift again.

That is wrong.

Once you receive the gift of tongues, it is yours, and you can exercise it at your will, which you should do regularly — especially when you pray. But that does not mean that you have the gift of speaking out in tongues in a worship service, which would require interpretation so that everyone who hears can understand the message and be edified by it.

According to Dake, "This is why the vocal gifts of prophecy, tongues, and interpretation of tongues is commanded to be regulated and even judged as to whether it be under direct inspiration or whether the person is exercising a gift of himself."[3]

We must remember that a distinction occurs between tongues as a prayer language and a message from God that is delivered through tongues and interpretation in a worship service.

Why Speak in Tongues?

"Whoever believes in me, as the Scripture has said, streams of living water will flow from within him."

By this he meant the Spirit, whom those who believed in him were later to receive. . . .

John 7:38,39 NIV

In this passage Jesus was speaking of the Holy Spirit, Who had not yet been poured out upon believers. When He spoke of the "streams of living water" that would flow from anyone who believed in Him, I believe He was referring to the spiritual language that should be flowing from each of us who have received the fullness of the Holy Spirit.[4]

Some people say that speaking in tongues is for some believers but not for all. Although it is true that not all believers speak or pray in tongues, I believe all of them could, if they would. As we have seen, all of the believers present in the Upper Room spoke in tongues on the Day of Pentecost, and I believe all believers today can and should do the same.

Why don't all believers speak in tongues today as they did at Pentecost? I don't believe it is because they can't; I believe they are afraid to because they have been taught not to or they think tongues may be nothing but emotion.

While it is true that some believers are baptized in the Holy Spirit and do not speak in tongues, I don't believe that is God's best for them. If God has poured out His Holy Spirit upon you, I encourage you to receive all the spiritual gifts and abilities He wants to impart to you. God has made them available to you, so you should want to receive them in their fullness.

But *why* should all believers receive and exercise the gift of tongues?

As we saw in 1 Corinthians 14:2, when we speak in tongues, we are speaking secrets and mysteries to God. We are saying things in a spiritual language that our enemy Satan cannot understand.

We are also edifying ourselves, as we see in Jude 20: *But you, beloved, build yourselves up [founded] on your most holy faith [make progress, rise like an edifice higher and higher], praying in the Holy Spirit.*

When we speak in tongues, often we are prophesying great things over our lives, things that we might not be able to accept if we understood what we were saying.

Finally, when we pray in tongues, we are assured that we are praying as we should because the Holy Spirit is praying through us . . . *in our behalf with unspeakable yearnings and groanings too deep for utterance.*[5]

I want to encourage you not to be afraid of the Holy Spirit and His gifts just because you may not have experienced them. When you ask Him to give you one of His gifts, He will never give you a bad one. To be very honest, these things are hard to explain to anyone who has not experienced them, but once you have experienced them, there is no denying the reality of this wonderful gift of the baptism of the Holy Spirit.

Tongues as a Wonderful Gift

I thank God that I speak in [strange] tongues (languages) more than any of you or all of you put together.

1 Corinthians 14:18

This passage tells us that Paul was grateful for the wonderful privilege of praying in tongues, and he practiced it a great deal in his life.

So should you and I. Once we are baptized in the Holy Spirit, we can speak or pray in tongues anytime we choose. We don't have to wait for some special feeling to come over us and move us to do so. Just as we can pray in our native tongue anytime we choose, we can pray in tongues anytime we choose, but the two ways of praying are not the same.

In 1 Corinthians 14:15 Paul clearly shows that praying with the spirit (by the Holy Spirit) is not the same as praying with the understanding: *Then what am I to do? I will pray with my spirit [by the Holy Spirit that is within me], but I will also pray [intelligently] with my mind and understanding. . . .* The great apostle Paul said that he prayed with his mind or understanding, but he also prayed with his spirit.

Of course, it is possible to pray Spirit-led prayers in your own native language, and that is a valuable and right thing to do. But that is not what Paul was talking about in this verse. When he said he prayed with his spirit, he meant that he prayed in other tongues.

Have Tongues Passed Away?

. . . As for prophecy (the gift of interpreting the divine will and purpose), it will be fulfilled and pass away; as for tongues, they will be destroyed and cease; as for knowledge, it will pass away [it will lose its value and be superseded by truth].

1 Corinthians 13:8

Some people and even some churches teach that the gift of speaking in tongues has passed away. They base this argument on Paul's first letter to the Corinthians in which he said that one day the spiritual gifts would no longer exist.

However, we know that prophecy and knowledge have not passed away. Those gifts are accepted today by almost all believers and are practiced in some form in almost all churches. Knowledge is sought for worldwide. It certainly has not passed away. Why then should we believe that the spiritual gift of tongues has passed away?

One reason some believers and some churches are opposed to speaking in tongues is that they have seen them abused or misused. But that is nothing new. The same thing was happening in Paul's day.[6] That is why he wrote to the believers in Corinth, instructing them in what he considered the proper operation of the gifts of the Spirit, including speaking in tongues.

In 1 Corinthians 14:40 KJV, Paul instructed the Corinthians on how the spiritual gift of tongues should be exercised in the church service — *decently and in order.* But nowhere did he say that this gift had passed away or that it should not be received and exercised by all believers. In fact, in *The Amplified Bible* translation of verse 39 he said, . . . *do not forbid or hinder speaking in [unknown] tongues.*

Yes, Paul found excess in the exercise of the gift of tongues, and he dealt with it. But he did not command or even suggest that tongues should be done away with to get rid of the excess.

Some people teach against things they don't understand or have not personally experienced. This is sad and robs many people of God's fullness for them.

Each of the gifts of the Holy Spirit is important and each has a role to play in the life of the believer. These gifts are bestowed upon us for a reason and a purpose. Open your heart to the Lord in faith and trust, allowing Him not only to fill you with His Holy Spirit, but also to impart to you the particular gifts He wants you to have — including the gift of tongues.

8
THE GIFTS AND THE
MOTIVATION OF LOVE

8
THE GIFTS AND THE MOTIVATION OF LOVE

~

But earnestly desire and zealously cultivate the greatest and best gifts and graces (the higher gifts and the choicest graces). And yet I will show you a still more excellent way [one that is better by far and the highest of them all — love].

1 Corinthians 12:31

With this verse Paul concludes Chapter 12, stating that while we need to be aware of the gifts of the Spirit and know that they are available to us, our motivation for seeking the baptism of the Holy Spirit is to be love. God wants to give us power through the baptism of the Holy Spirit so we can have a strong love walk and be a blessing to others.

Pursue Love

Eagerly pursue and seek to acquire [this] love [make it your aim, your great quest]; and earnestly desire and cultivate the spiritual endowments (gifts), especially that you may prophesy (interpret the divine will and purpose in inspired preaching and teaching).

1 Corinthians 14:1

Again, Paul's point is that although we are to seek and develop the gifts of the Spirit, our main goal should be love.

As we saw in the first verse of 1 Corinthians 13, Paul wrote that even if we can speak in the tongues of men and of angels, but do not have love, we are nothing but a big noise.

Although we have talked about tongues in this book, I don't want you to think that just speaking in tongues is everything there is to the baptism of the Holy Spirit because we can speak in tongues and still just be a big noise, as the Bible says. We also need a desire to walk in love and to manifest good fruit — the fruit of the Holy Spirit.

This fruit is described in Galatians 5:22,23: *But the fruit of the [Holy] Spirit [the work which His presence within accomplishes] is love, joy (gladness), peace, patience (an even temper, forbearance), kindness, goodness (benevolence), faithfulness, gentleness (meekness, humility), self-control (self-restraint, continence). Against such things there is no law [that can bring a charge].*

Notice in verse 22 that the very first fruit of the Holy Spirit is *love.* I believe love is the primary fruit of the Spirit, and the others are all expressions of love. When we are baptized in the Holy Spirit, *we are totally filled with God's love for us and are able to minister to all those He sends our way.*

All of us are presented with a variety of opportunities to manifest love and the other spiritual fruit every day of our lives. Through the infilling of the Spirit, we have God's power, ability and strength to help us manifest these fruit with ease, which would otherwise be hard. There is no such thing as power without a strong love life.[1] When we walk in the love of God, everything else falls in line.

Tongues and Edification

He who speaks in a [strange] tongue edifies and improves himself, but he who prophesies [interpreting the divine will and purpose and teaching with inspiration] edifies and improves the church and promotes growth [in Christian wisdom, piety, holiness, and happiness].

1 Corinthians 14:4

After stressing the nature and importance of love in 1 Corinthians 13, in the fourteenth chapter, Paul returns to the subject of the gifts of the Holy Spirit, concentrating on the gift of tongues.

Although we have already discussed tongues, let's look at one more aspect of it.

As previously mentioned, the person who speaks in tongues speaks not to men but to God because no one understands our prayer language but the Holy Spirit. So unless the message they deliver in tongues is interpreted for the sake of others, the only person who is edified and improved is the person themselves.[2]

Paul makes this point clear later on in verse 13 of this same chapter when he writes: *Therefore, the person who speaks in an [unknown] tongue should pray [for*

*the power] to interpret and explain what
he says.*

In verse 14 he then goes on to explain:
*For if I pray in an [unknown] tongue, my
spirit [by the Holy Spirit within me]
prays, but my mind is unproductive [it
bears no fruit and helps nobody].*

If that is the case, if no one else is helped
by our praying in tongues, what should
we do? Paul gives the answer to that
question in verse 15: . . . *I will pray with
my spirit [by the Holy Spirit that is within
me], but I will also pray [intelligently]
with my mind and understanding; I will
sing with my spirit [by the Holy Spirit that
is within me], but I will sing [intelligently]
with my mind and understanding also.*

That is what I do. I pray and sing with my spirit in tongues, and I also pray and sing with my mind and understanding; I believe what I pray or sing in English afterward is the interpretation. When I pray and sing in tongues, whether or not I interpret it in English, I am still edified. But when praying and singing in tongues around others, such as in a worship service, you and I should do as Paul teaches — speak in tongues but also pray that we may interpret what we say. That way we are all edified.

Paul teaches that we are to keep the gifts of the Spirit, particularly speaking in tongues, in balance. We are to operate in them properly, especially in the midst of a congregation of people.

Whenever we pray in tongues, we are assured that we are praying as we should because the Holy Spirit is praying through us.

Help of the Spirit in Prayer

So too the [Holy] Spirit comes to our aid and bears us up in our weakness; for we do not know what prayer to offer nor how to offer it worthily as we ought, but the Spirit Himself goes to meet our supplication and pleads in our behalf with unspeakable yearnings and groanings too deep for utterance.

Romans 8:26

This verse teaches us that the Holy Spirit assists us in prayer by helping us to pray as we ought to. If we will allow Him to do so, He will pray through us the perfect prayer with yearnings and groanings that are unutterable.

Sometimes when we are praying in the Spirit, all we get from the Holy Spirit is, "Oh, God!" or just a groaning or utterances or speaking in other tongues, but we can be assured that we're praying the perfect prayer that's going to get the job done because . . . *He Who searches the hearts of men knows what is in the mind of the [Holy] Spirit [what His intent is], because the Spirit intercedes and pleads [before God] in behalf of the saints according to and in harmony with God's will.*[3]

Just think about it — if you and I are believers in Jesus Christ, we are the

home of the Holy Spirit of God, and He
is making intercession to our heavenly
Father on our behalf twenty-four hours
a day, seven days a week! This truth
should make us bold, fearless and
aggressive in a balanced way. We should
believe we can do whatever we need to
do that is part of God's plan for us
because we are equipped through the
power of the Holy Spirit. With Him, we
have what we need and more besides to
live a victorious life.

The Holy Spirit is our guarantee of the
good things that are to come. I believe
God desires to take you to new heights
in Him through the power of His Spirit.
I encourage you to throw yourself
entirely open to Him and ask the Holy

Spirit to get involved in every area of your life. If you will do that in honesty and sincerity, He will begin to work in you in a powerful and exciting way.

Conclusion: Receive the Holy Spirit!

Conclusion: Receive the Holy Spirit!

~

*Then Jesus said to them again, Peace to you!
[Just] as the Father has sent Me forth, so I am
sending you.*

*And having said this, He breathed on them
and said to them, Receive the Holy Spirit!*

John 20:21,22

In these pages I have tried to reveal to
you how the limitless power of God is
manifested in our life through the
baptism of the Holy Spirit and how it is
central to experiencing true success in
everything we do. You will gain the most

value from reading this book if you have already received the fullness of the Holy Spirit, or if you go on to receive it. So, if you haven't already done so, I hope that you will open the channel for God to begin to move in your life in a mighty and powerful way by asking for the baptism of the Holy Spirit.[1]

But, if at this point, you are undecided as to whether or not you want to receive it, may I encourage you to do something? Put this book down and take some time to pray about it and think about it. Study the Bible for yourself and let God speak a word of confirmation to you in your heart.

If you would like to receive the baptism of the Holy Spirit and the spiritual gifts He wants to bestow on you, just open your heart to the Lord and pray this prayer in faith and sincerity:

Lord Jesus, You are the Baptizer, the One Who baptizes in the Holy Spirit, and I am asking You right now to baptize me in the power of the Holy Spirit with the evidence of speaking in tongues.

Pour out Your Spirit upon me, Lord. Fill every part of my being so that I am flooded with Your power and Presence.

Give me the spiritual gifts that You want to bestow upon me so that I can be equipped and empowered to minister to others in need.

Thank You for Your marvelous love. Help me to share it with all those with whom I come in contact day by day.

All this I pray in Your precious, holy name. Amen.

Begin to Speak in Tongues

And they were all filled with the Holy Spirit and began to speak with other tongues, as the Spirit gave them utterance.

Acts 2:4 NKJV

Now open your mouth in faith and begin to speak in other tongues. Don't be afraid. Utter those little syllables that come to you.

Your mind may be unfruitful, but this kind of language does not come from the head; it comes from the inner man.

Don't try to figure it out, just release it in Jesus' name.

You may have received only a little bit of language, but don't let that stop you. I encourage you to continue to use what you have received, and you will receive more.

Remember, when I first began to speak in tongues, I only had four words, and the enemy tried to tell me that I had nothing, that I was just making it up. He will try to tell you the same thing. Don't listen to him. Keep speaking as the Spirit gives you utterance. Sooner or later it will grow into an entire language, just as it did for me.

If you did not begin to speak in your prayer language for some reason, don't be discouraged. If you asked in faith and sincerity, I believe you did receive the baptism of the Holy Spirit. The power of the Holy Spirit is flowing through you right now. In your private time with God continue to offer your voice to Him, and in faith utter any syllables that may come to you.

If you would like to know more about the baptism and ministry of the Holy Spirit, I encourage you to begin studying and finding out all you can on the subject. To help get you started, there is a recommended reading list on the Spirit-filled life at the back of this book.

If you did receive the baptism of the Holy Spirit through this book, I would appreciate it if you would contact our office at the address and telephone number also listed in the back so we may rejoice with you.

I pray that you have been blessed by this book and that it has made a difference in your life. I am so excited about sharing these truths with you because the indwelling Holy Spirit is such a great blessing. He inspires us to do great things. He endues us with power for all of our tasks. He has been given to us to accomplish a whole series of things in us, through us and for us.

The Holy Spirit is in you not only to help you retain these truths, but to give you many others besides. Begin to apply what you have read, and *enjoy your new life in the Spirit!*

ENDNOTES

ENDNOTES

Introduction

[1] See John 14:16.

[2] See Acts 2:38.

Chapter 1

[1] Spiros Zodhiates, Th.D., *The Complete Word Study Dictionary: New Testament* (Chattanooga: AMG Publishers, 1992), s.v. "baptize."

[2] *New Unger's Bible Dictionary* originally published by Moody Press of Chicago, Illinois. Copyright © 1988. Used by permission, s.v. "PROPHET."

[3] See Luke 3:16.

[4] See Colossians 2:9,10.

Chapter 2

[1] See John 14:20,23.

[2] See Romans 15:16.

[3] See Philippians 1:6.

Chapter 3

[1] James Strong, *The Exhaustive Concordance of the Bible* (Nashville: Abingdon Press, 1978), p. 25, #1411.

[2] *Nelson's Illustrated Bible Dictionary.* Copyright © 1986 by Thomas Nelson Publishers. All rights reserved. Used by permission; s.v. "Power."

[3] Romans 8:29.

[4] John 20:22.

[5] ". . . Man's spirit was originally the highest part of his entire being to which soul and body were to be subject. . . ." Watchman Nee, *The Spiritual Man,* (New York: Christian Fellowship Publishers, Inc., 1968), p. 43.

[6] ". . . The immediate effect of sin on Adam and Eve was that they died spiritually and became subject to spiritual death. . . ." Lewis Sperry Chafer, Revised by John F. Walvoord, *Major*

Bible Themes, (Grand Rapids, Michigan: Academie Books from Zondervan Publishing House, 1974), p. 174.

7 *Dictionary of Pentecostal and Charismatic Movements,* Eds. Stanley M. Burgess and Gary B. McGee (Grand Rapids, Michigan: Zondervan Publishing House, Copyright © 1988), pp. 2-3.

8 Acts 2:12.

9 See Galatians 4:7; Ephesians 1:11-14.

Chapter 4

1 Pat Boone, *A New Song,* (Carol Stream, Illinois: Creation House, August, 1970), pp. 126-129.

Chapter 5

1 2 Corinthians 3:18 KJV.

Chapter 6

1 *Dictionary of Pentecostal and Charismatic Movements,* pp. 890-892, "WISDOM, WORD OF."

2   *Dictionary of Pentecostal and Charismatic Movements*, pp. 527-528, "KNOWLEDGE, WORD OF."

3   Arnold Bittlinger, *Gifts and Graces*, (Grand Rapids, Michigan: William B. Eerdmans Publishing Company, Copyright © 1967), pp. 32-34, "(c) *The Gift of Faith*."

4   Mark 16:17,18.

5   Gordon D. Fee, *God's Empowering Presence*, (Peabody, Massachusetts: Hendrickson Publishers, Copyright © 1994), pp. 168-169, "(3) *Faith*," "(4) *Gifts of Healings*."

6   See Romans 12:3 KJV.

7   *Gifts and Graces*, pp. 42-45, "(f) The Gift of Prophecy."

8   See Acts 16:16-18.

9   The discerning of divine spirits can be seen in such Scripture passages as Exodus 33:18-34:7 when Moses looked into the spirit realm and saw the "back parts" of God and in Revelation 1:9-20 when John was in exile on the isle of Patmos and had a vision of the throne of God.

10. *Matthew Henry's Commentary on the Whole Bible: New Modern Edition,* Electronic Database. Copyright © 1991 by Hendrickson Publishers, Inc. Used by permission. All rights reserved, "1 Corinthians 12:1-11."

11. Dennis and Rita Bennett, *The Holy Spirit and You,* (South Plainfield, New Jersey: Bridge Publishing, Inc., 1971), p. 143, "Discerning of Spirits."

Chapter 7

1. Finis Jennings Dake, *Dake's Annotated Reference Bible,* (Lawrenceville, Georgia: Dake Bible Sales, Inc., Copyright © 1963), p. 123, "The Acts 2, r."

2. *Dake's,* p. 123, "The Acts 2, r."

3. *Dake's,* p. 123, "The Acts 2, r."

4. ". . . The Jews frequently compare the gifts and influences of the Holy Spirit to water in general — to rain, fountains, wells, rivers, etc., . . ." *Clarke's Commentary,* by Adam Clarke, Electronic Database. Copyright © 1996 by Biblesoft. All rights reserved, "John 7:38."

[5] Romans 8:26.

[6] *Matthew Henry's Commentary on the Whole Bible: New Modern Edition,* "1 Corinthians 12:1-11, On spiritual gifts."

Chapter 8

[1] See Ephesians 3:17-19.

[2] See Jude 20.

[3] Romans 8:27.

Conclusion

[1] Luke 11:13.

Recommended Reading

Bennett, Dennis J., *Nine O'clock in the Morning*. Plainfield, New Jersey: Logos International, 1970.

Frost, Robert C., Ph.D., *Aglow with the Spirit*. Plainfield, New Jersey: Logos International, 1965.

Sherrill, John L., *They Speak with Other Tongues*. New York, Toronto, London: McGraw-Hill Book Company, 1964.

About the Author

Joyce Meyer has been teaching the Word of God since 1976 and in full-time ministry since 1980. Previously the associate pastor at Life Christian Center in St. Louis, Missouri, she developed, coordinated, and taught a weekly meeting known as "Life In The Word." After more than five years, the Lord brought it to a conclusion, directing her to establish her own ministry and call it *"Life In The Word, Inc."*

Now, her *Life In The Word* radio and television broadcasts are seen and heard by millions across the United States and throughout the world. Joyce's teaching tapes are enjoyed internationally, and she travels extensively conducting *Life In The Word* conferences.

Joyce and her husband, Dave, the business administrator at *Life In The Word,* have been married for over 34 years. They reside in St. Louis, Missouri, and are the parents of four children. All four children are married and, along with their spouses, work with Dave and Joyce in the ministry.

Believing the call on her life is to establish believers in God's Word, Joyce says, "Jesus died to set the captives free, and far too many Christians have little or no victory in their daily lives." Finding herself in the same situation many years ago and having found freedom to live in victory through applying God's Word, Joyce goes equipped to set captives free and to exchange ashes for beauty. She believes that every person who walks in victory leads many others into victory. Her life is transparent, and her teachings are practical and can be applied in everyday life.

Joyce has taught on emotional healing and related subjects in meetings all over the country, helping multiplied thousands. She has recorded more than 225 different audiocassette albums and over 70 videos. She has also authored 46 books to help the body of Christ on various topics.

Her "Emotional Healing Package" contains over 23 hours of teaching on the subject. Albums included in this package are: "Confidence"; "Beauty for Ashes" (includes a syllabus — Joyce's teaching notes); "Managing Your Emotions"; "Bitterness, Resentment, and Unforgiveness"; "Root of Rejection"; and a 90-minute Scripture/music tape titled "Healing the Brokenhearted."

Joyce's "Mind Package" features five different audio tape series on the subject of the mind. They include: "Mental Strongholds and Mindsets"; "Wilderness Mentality"; "The Mind of the Flesh"; "The Wandering, Wondering Mind"; and "Mind, Mouth, Moods, and Attitudes." The package also contains

Joyce's powerful book, *Battlefield of the Mind.* On the subject of love she has three tape series titled "Love Is..."; "Love: The Ultimate Power"; and "Loving God, Loving Yourself, and Loving Others," and a book titled *Reduce Me to Love.*

Write to Joyce Meyer's office for a resource catalog and further information on how to obtain the tapes you need to bring total healing to your life.

To contact the author write:
Joyce Meyer Ministries
P. O. Box 655
Fenton, Missouri 63026
or call: (636) 349-0303

Internet Address: www.joycemeyer.org

Please include your testimony or help received from this book when you write. Your prayer requests are welcome.

To contact the author
in Canada, please write:
Joyce Meyer Ministries Canada, Inc.
Lambeth Box 1300
London, ON N6P 1T5
or call: (636) 349-0303

In Australia, please write:
Joyce Meyer Ministries-Australia
Locked Bag 77
Mansfield Delivery Centre
Queensland 4122
or call: (07) 3349 1200

In England, please write:
Joyce Meyer Ministries
P. O. Box 1549
Windsor
SL4 1GT
or call: 01753 831102

BOOKS BY JOYCE MEYER

Filled with the Spirit

A Celebration of Simplicity

The Joy of Believing Prayer

Never Lose Heart

Being the Person God Made You to Be

A Leader in the Making

"Good Morning, This Is God!" Gift Book

JESUS — Name Above All Names

"Good Morning, This Is God!" Daily Calendar

Help Me — I'm Married!

Reduce Me to Love

Be Healed in Jesus' Name

How to Succeed at Being Yourself

Eat and Stay Thin

Weary Warriors, Fainting Saints

Life in the Word Journal

Life in the Word Devotional

Be Anxious for Nothing

The Help Me! Series:
I'm Alone!
I'm Stressed! • I'm Insecure!
I'm Discouraged! • I'm Depressed!
I'm Worried! • I'm Afraid!

Don't Dread

Managing Your Emotions

Healing the Brokenhearted

THE HARRISON HOUSE VISION

Proclaiming the truth and the power

Of the Gospel of Jesus Christ

With excellence;

Challenging Christians to

Live victoriously,

Grow spiritually,

Know God intimately.